THE CREATIVE COOK

For The Love

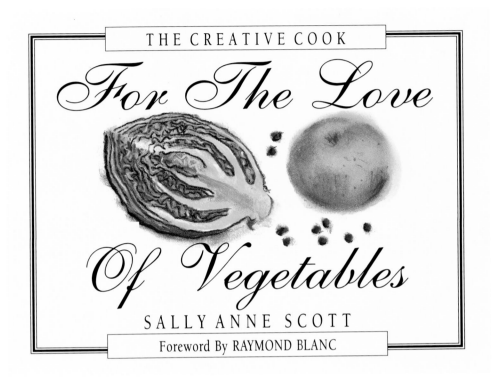

Of Vegetables

SALLY ANNE SCOTT

Foreword By RAYMOND BLANC

COLE
GROUP

To Montse especially, and to Freddie for
his understanding

Please note the following:

Quantities given in all the recipes serve 4 people unless otherwise stated.

Butter and margarine are packaged in a variety of forms, including 1-pound blocks and ¼-pound sticks. A stick equals 8 tablespoons (½ cup).

Cream used is specified as light cream (containing from 18 percent to 30 percent milk fat), whipping cream (30 percent to 36 percent milk fat), or heavy cream (at least 36 percent milk fat).

Flour used is all-purpose flour, unless otherwise specified.

Preparation of ingredients, such as the cleaning, trimming, and peeling of vegetables and fruit, is presumed and the text refers to any aspect of this only if unusual, such as onions used unpeeled, etc.

Citrus fruit should be thoroughly washed to remove any agricultural residues. For this reason, whenever a recipe uses the rind of any citrus such as oranges, lemon, or limes, the text specifies washed fruit. Wash the fruit thoroughly, rinse well, and pat dry. If using organically grown fruit, rinse briefly and pat dry.

Eggs used are large unless otherwise specified. Because of the risk of contamination with salmonella bacteria, current recommendations from health professionals are that children, pregnant women, people on immuno-suppressant drugs, and the elderly should not eat raw or lightly cooked eggs. This book includes recipes with raw and lightly cooked eggs. These recipes are marked by an ★ in the text.

Editorial Direction: Lewis Esson Publishing
Art Director: Mary Evans
Design: Peter Butler
Illustrations: Alison Barratt
Food for Photography: Meg Jansz
Styling: Debbie Patterson
Editorial Assistant: Penny David
American Editor: Norma MacMillan
Production: Alison McIver

Published in 1994 by Cole Group
4415 Sonoma Highway/PO Box 4089
Santa Rosa, CA 95402-4089
(800) 959-2717   (707) 538-0492
Fax (707) 538-0497

First published in 1992 by
Conran Octopus Limited,
37 Shelton Street, London WC2H 9HN

A   B   C   D   E   F   G   H
4   5   6   7   8   9   0   1

ISBN 1-56426-656-7

Library of Congress Catalog Number 93-39686

Typeset by Servis Filmsetting Ltd
Printed and bound in Hong Kong

Distributed to the book trade by Publishers Group West

CONTENTS

FOREWORD

My roots are firmly embedded in the soil of rural France. In a small country village in Franche-Comté, I received an education in real food. I learned very early on that vegetables are Nature's bounty and to appreciate the endless variety that followed the almost magical rhythm of the seasons. As in any French country garden, nine-tenths of the area would be devoted to vegetables and only one-tenth to flowers. My father's regular offerings to my mother would be great bunches of carrots and parsley, which she would then transform using her traditional skills to create so much happiness around the table.

At *Le Manoir aux Quat' Saisons*, my restaurant near Oxford, England, we have endeavored to recreate this natural environment. Our *potager*, or kitchen garden, is not a gimmick but plays an important role in the excellence of the establishment. Using organic techniques, we grow at least 70 varieties of vegetables, 17 types of salad leaves, and 110 different herbs. From the selection of the seeds and their planting, through the growing and harvesting, much care is devoted to the plants and this produces immense rewards in wonderful tasty produce.

Whether or not you are lucky enough to grow your own produce, *For the Love of Vegetables* gives you a wide range of ideas of the best ways to make the most of the incredible range of tastes and textures they offer.

You will also find the recipes in this book very easy to follow, so you won't have to slave for hours in the kitchen in order to produce a good meal. Instead you will rediscover the unique pleasure obtained from creating a new dish, and the joy obtained from sharing it with others. The whole process should be easy and fun, from planning and shopping to cooking and presenting the dish at the table. Your efforts will be well rewarded by the appreciative response of your family and friends. *Bon appetit!*

RAYMOND BLANC

INTRODUCTION

More and more people now seem ready to accept that "we are what we eat," hence today's new degree of interest in healthy eating. With that in mind, there has been a great shift in emphasis away from high-fat, high-cholesterol, meat-centered meals toward a greater consumption of vegetables, which as well as being low in fat and cholesterol and high in fiber are also bursting with vitamins, minerals, and other nutrients – some of which are not just simply "good for you," but active agents in preventing disease.

Another reason for the current enthusiasm for vegetables is the sheer availability of so many varieties – old and new. With the vast increase in international trade – and improved refrigeration and storage techniques in food distribution – there is now little that cannot be obtained readily almost all year round. Varied and interesting selections are stacked invitingly on supermarket shelves, – even, in some cases, with details of how best they can be used.

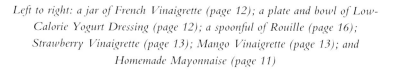

Left to right: a jar of French Vinaigrette (page 12); a plate and bowl of Low-Calorie Yogurt Dressing (page 12); a spoonful of Rouille (page 16); Strawberry Vinaigrette (page 13); Mango Vinaigrette (page 13); and Homemade Mayonnaise (page 11)

Since we are now no longer bound by the seasons, it is always possible to create exciting, economical, and different food. Almost on a daily basis, we see the steady signs of merging world cultures and cuisines. This brings the possibility of exploring new tastes and ideas, particularly from traditions like those of the Mediterranean and Asia in which vegetables are given much more prominence. From such learning we may then make adaptations to suit both our own palates and our ways of cooking and eating.

BUYING AND STORING VEGETABLES

To get the full benefit of the flavor and nutritional value of a vegetable, it should be bought and used as fresh as possible. Try to buy little and often, and from a reputable supplier with a rapid turnover.

Color and firmness are the best indications of freshness. Dull exteriors and limp leaves indicate vegetables have languished on the shelf too long. Avoid any that are blemished or too soft – or too hard! Wherever possible, buy as whole and intact a plant as possible, as it then bears better clues as to age. For instance, the green tops on a root vegetable like a carrot wither very quickly, although the root itself takes weeks to show any visible signs of fading. If you can, break a leaf or stem; it should snap cleanly and have some drops of moisture on it.

In my opinion, organic produce wins hands-down in terms of fuller flavor and nutritional content. If organic vegetables and salad leaves are not available, do scrub others particularly thoroughly to remove any lingering chemicals.

Once you have your vegetables home, storage there is also important. Keep roots, like potatoes, onions, carrots, etc., loosely wrapped, in cool, dark, airy places (not in the refrigerator, or they lose texture). Stem, leaf, and fruiting vegetables are best kept in the refrigerator, wrapped in plastic bags to prevent dehydration. Some plants, especially herbs, can be kept like flowers in pitchers of water.

PREPARING AND COOKING VEGETABLES

When preparing vegetables, try to do as little to them as possible. For instance, try to leave intact any edible skins, such as those of cucumbers, summer squash, and new potatoes, as they are particularly rich in flavor and nutrients. Also, try to do any peeling and cutting as near to cooking time as possible, as vegetables left soaking in water rapidly lose their nutrients to it – along with their flavor.

For the same reason cooking times should generally be as short as possible. This not only preserves flavor and nutrients but helps keep bright colors. Of course, the degree of tenderness of vegetables is a very personal thing. I like mine crunchy to get the benefit of their texture, but cooking times in the recipes can be adjusted to suit personal preference.

With this in mind, speedy cooking methods such as sautéing and stir-frying are preferable to lengthy boiling and stewing. Methods like steaming and grilling have the additional advantage of employing little or no cooking medium either to add fat or to leach away flavor and goodness. When boiling vegetables, try to remember to put the cooking water to use as a stock for further cooking.

The revolution in our supermarkets and grocers has also given us much more interesting ingredients with which to cook and dress vegetables and salads. Consider the huge variety of oils now available. As well as the wide range of tasty olive oils, there are the highly flavored nut oils like hazelnut, walnut, and toasted sesame, as well as the healthy vegetable oils such as corn and sunflower whose delicate flavors are excellent in dishes where the other flavors need no competition.

The versatility of vegetables and salads is endless. Be bold with the combinations and bear in mind that color, texture, and taste are everything. My recipes will – I hope – be an inspiration for those who have not yet had the courage to try new ways with vegetables. Have fun with food!

VEGETABLE STOCK

MAKES ABOUT 1 QUART

1 cup dried navy beans, soaked in cold water overnight
3 tbsp butter
1 tbsp sunflower or canola oil
1 garlic clove
1 stalk of celery
6 carrots, coarsely chopped
3 leeks, coarsely chopped
3 turnips, cubed
2 onions
12 whole cloves
1 parsnip
small sprig of fresh thyme
3 bay leaves
small bunch of fresh parsley
salt and freshly ground black pepper

Drain the navy beans, rinse, and put them in a saucepan. Cover them with fresh cold water and bring to a boil. Drain, rinse, and cover with more fresh cold water. Bring to a boil again and then drain.

Melt the butter with the oil in a large heavy pan over medium heat. Sauté the garlic 2 minutes.

Add the celery, carrots, leeks, turnips, onions with the cloves, and the parsnip. Cook 5–7 minutes, stirring constantly.

Remove from the heat and add the drained beans, followed by 3 quarts of water, the thyme, bay leaves, and the parsley, complete with stems. Bring to a boil, cover, and simmer gently 1½ hours.

Remove from the heat and let cool about 2 hours.

Return the pan to low heat and simmer 15 minutes. Strain the stock, return it to the pan, and boil rapidly to reduce it by about half.

Cool any stock not being used immediately and then store it in the refrigerator.

BASIC BOUILLON OR ENRICHED MEAT STOCK

MAKES ABOUT 3½ CUPS

1½–2lb beef shank
carcass of 1 fresh chicken
1 onion, coarsely chopped
3 carrots, coarsely chopped
bouquet garni
2 stalks of celery, coarsely chopped
8 black peppercorns

Chop the meat and chicken into manageable pieces and place them in a large pan. Cover with 2¼ quarts of cold water and bring to a boil.

Reduce the heat and add the other ingredients. Cover and cook gently about 1½ hours, skimming as necessary.

Remove all the larger solids from the pan, then strain the stock through a cheesecloth-lined strainer.

Return the liquid to the heat and boil it rapidly to reduce it by about half. Strain it through cheesecloth again before use.

Cool any stock not being used immediately and then store it in the refrigerator.

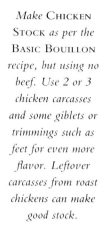

Make CHICKEN STOCK *as per the* BASIC BOUILLON *recipe, but using no beef. Use 2 or 3 chicken carcasses and some giblets or trimmings such as feet for even more flavor. Leftover carcasses from roast chickens can make good stock.*

Make FISH STOCK
*with 1 ½ lb of fish
heads and
trimmings, 3
onions, 3 bay
leaves, and a bunch
of parsley. Cover
with water, bring to
a boil, and simmer
20 minutes only.*

Variations on
BÉCHAMEL *include*
AURORE SAUCE,
*which contains
added tomato pulp
or purée and*
MORNAY, *which is
flavored with grated
cheese.*

QUICK TOMATO SAUCE

MAKES ABOUT 1 CUP

*¼ cup olive oil
2 garlic cloves, minced
1 tbsp finely chopped parsley
small pinch of red pepper flakes
one 14-oz can tomatoes
salt and freshly ground black pepper*

Heat the oil over medium heat and cook the garlic, parsley, and red pepper flakes stirring constantly, until soft, 1–2 minutes.

 Crush or purèe the tomatoes and add to the pan. Bring to a boil, season to taste, mix well, and remove from heat.

BÉCHAMEL SAUCE

MAKES ABOUT 1¼ CUPS

*1 ¼ cups milk
1 small onion
¼ tsp freshly grated nutmeg
1 bay leaf
sprig of fresh thyme
2 tbsp butter
2 tbsp flour
salt and freshly ground black pepper*

Place the milk in a saucepan together with the onion, nutmeg, bay leaf, and thyme. Very slowly bring a boil. Immediately remove from the heat and let infuse 20 minutes.

 Melt the butter in a heavy saucepan. Stir in the flour and cook thoroughly, stirring constantly, about 4 minutes.

 Strain the infused milk and then gradually add it to the butter and flour in the pan. Mix thoroughly and then bring to a boil, stirring constantly.

 Reduce the heat and simmer 3–4 minutes, still stirring. Season with salt and pepper and a little more nutmeg, if desired.

HOLLANDAISE SAUCE★

MAKES ABOUT 1¼ CUPS

14 tbsp unsalted butter
3 egg yolks
(★see page 2 for advice on eggs)
1 tbsp lemon juice
1 tbsp dry white wine
salt and freshly ground black pepper

Melt 12 tbsp of the butter in a heavy pan over low heat. Transfer to a warmed measuring cup.

Place the egg yolks in the same pan and beat them quickly with a whisk. Add half the lemon juice, the wine, and a pinch of salt. Beat again. Add half the remaining unmelted butter and place the pan in a water bath or double boiler.

Whisking steadily, cook gently until the egg yolks are creamy in texture and beginning to thicken. Immediately remove the pan from heat and stir in the remaining unmelted butter until it is all absorbed.

Dribble the melted butter into the yolk mixture, whisking fast. Add the butter more rapidly as the sauce thickens. When the sauce is the consistency of thick cream, add the remaining lemon juice and adjust the seasoning.

Notes: If the sauce is too thick, it can be thinned with 1 tablespoon of water.

Hollandaise not being used immediately should be stored in the refrigerator a day or two only.

Try adding 3 tablespoons of freshly grated Parmesan cheese to the sauce for extra flavor.

HOMEMADE MAYONNAISE★

MAKES ABOUT 1 CUP

1 egg yolk
(★see page 2 for advice on eggs)
½ tsp salt
½ tsp dry mustard
freshly ground black pepper
⅔ cup olive oil
1 tbsp white wine vinegar or lemon juice
pinch of sugar (optional)

In a bowl beat the egg yolk until thick. Then beat in the salt, mustard, and black pepper to taste.

Add the oil very slowly, drop by drop, whisking constantly so the oil is absorbed evenly. When the mayonnaise thickens and becomes shiny, add the oil in a thin steady stream. Finally, blend in the vinegar or lemon juice and sugar, if using.

Notes: Any mayonnaise not being used immediately should be stored in the refrigerator a day or two only.

Try flavoring the mayonnaise with 2 or 3 garlic cloves, 2 tablespoons chopped fresh minced herbs, or 1 tablespoon grated orange or lemon zest.

Make BÉARNAISE SAUCE *in the same way as* HOLLANDAISE, *but first flavor the vinegar by boiling it with some chopped shallots, fresh tarragon, and black peppercorns.*

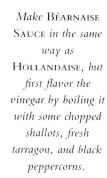

For really exciting salad dressings, use the wide variety of flavored oils and vinegars now readily available. As appropriate, more exotic items, such as nut oils – like sesame, walnut and hazelnut – soy sauce, tahini (sesame-seed paste), and Japanese rice vinegar are also very useful. It is also quite easy to make flavored oils and vinegars at home by adding flavoring ingredients such as fresh herbs like tarragon or rosemary, 3 or 4 garlic cloves, 1 or 2 small hot chili peppers, or some berry fruit to good-quality oil or white wine vinegar, and leaving it in a cool place several weeks.

LOW-CALORIE YOGURT DRESSING★

MAKES 2 CUPS

3 egg yolks
(★see page 2 for advice on eggs)
2 cups thick plain yogurt
2 tsp lime or lemon juice
2 tsp Dijon-style mustard
salt and freshly ground black pepper
1 tbsp minced fresh parsley

In a bowl, beat the egg yolks, yogurt, and lemon juice together until creamy.

Set the bowl in a pan of very gently simmering water and cook, stirring constantly, until the dressing has thickened to a coating consistency, about 15 minutes.

Add the mustard, season with salt and pepper, and let cool. Stir in the parsley just before use.

Store any not being used immediately in a screwtop jar in the refrigerator a day or two only.

FRENCH VINAIGRETTE

MAKES ABOUT ⅔ CUP

2–3 garlic cloves, minced
2 tbsp wine vinegar
2 tsp Dijon-style mustard
salt and freshly ground black pepper
pinch of sugar (optional)
6 tbsp olive oil

In a bowl, whisk together the minced garlic, vinegar, mustard, salt and pepper, and sugar, if using. Add the oil and whisk together well.

Note: Use more or less garlic to taste. Try flavoring the dressing with the additions as listed for Basic Vinaigrette.

BASIC VINAIGRETTE

MAKES ABOUT ⅔ CUP

6 tbsp olive oil
2 tbsp wine vinegar
salt and freshly ground black pepper

Pour the oil and vinegar into a screwtop jar. Seal and shake vigorously. Season and shake again.

Notes: Add 2 teaspoons of minced fresh herbs, such as parsley, chervil, or chives, for an herb vinaigrette.

Instead of these herbs, the vinaigrette can be flavored with 2 tablespoons of chopped fresh tarragon, 1 tablespoon of tomato paste with a pinch of paprika, 2 tablespoons each of minced onions and parsley, or 1 tablespoon of minced anchovy.

STRAWBERRY VINAIGRETTE

MAKES ABOUT ¾ CUP

⅓ cup strawberries
1 ½ tbsp strawberry vinegar or lemon juice
6 tbsp grapeseed oil
salt and freshly ground black pepper

Put the strawberries in a blender or food processor with the vinegar or lemon juice. Pulse briefly until the mixture is smooth.

With the machine running, gradually add the oil until it is all incorporated and the mixture is thick and smooth. Strain out the seeds, if desired. Season.

Note: Serve with a cucumber salad or with cold poached chicken or salmon.

MANGO VINAIGRETTE

MAKES ABOUT ¾ CUP

1 very ripe mango, peeled
1 ½ tbsp red wine vinegar or lemon juice
5 tbsp sunflower or canola oil
1 tbsp minced fresh parsley
salt and freshly ground black pepper

Slice the mango flesh coarsely from the seed.

Put the mango flesh in a blender or food processor with the vinegar or lemon juice. Pulse briefly until the mixture is smooth.

With the machine running, gradually add the oil until it is all incorporated and the mixture is thick and smooth. Stir in the parsley and season.

Note: Serve with smoked chicken salads, or flavor with chopped fresh dill or mint and serve with smoked fish. Try flavoring it with some mustard, too.

Left: Strawberry Vinaigrette; right: Mango Vinaigrette

SOUPS

Soups are perhaps the easiest way to make the most of vegetables. As they are cooked in the soup there is also minimal loss of flavor and nutrients. There are two golden rules for good soups. First, always use the freshest of vegetables; second, any stock used must be a good one – either make your own as per the recipes in the Introduction or buy a good-quality canned broth or bouillon. If you have to use bouillon cubes, remember they are usually highly seasoned, so go carefully with the salt. The flavor of a soup will also be improved if any water used is bottled spring water, or at least filtered tap water. I am known for my soups and like to serve large bowlfuls, so the quantities given are fairly generous. I also like my soups quite thick, but the consistencies can be adjusted with a little more stock, water, or cream as appropriate.

Left to right: Potato and Pumpkin Soup with Rouille (page 16); Chilled Sorrel Soup with Seafood (page 17); Golden Swedish Soup (page 16) garnished with chopped herbs

The strongly flavored Provençal sauce, ROUILLE, *is most usually served with fish and seafood soups and stews. It is best made with a little of the stock or soup it accompanies.*

POTATO AND PUMPKIN SOUP WITH ROUILLE★

SERVES 6–8

½ lb potatoes; cut into chunks
3-lb piece of pumpkin; cut into chunks
1 cup chopped onions
4 tbsp butter
2 cups milk
1 tbsp flour
½ tsp freshly grated nutmeg
salt and freshly ground black pepper
1 cup light cream
FOR THE ROUILLE
3-oz chunk of dry bread
1 egg yolk
(★see page 2 for advice on eggs)
2 large garlic cloves, minced
2 red sweet peppers, coarsely chopped
½ tsp cayenne pepper
pinch of saffron
6 tbsp extra virgin olive oil

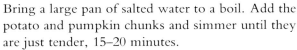

Bring a large pan of salted water to a boil. Add the potato and pumpkin chunks and simmer until they are just tender, 15–20 minutes.

Drain the vegetables, reserving the stock. Purée the vegetables in a blender or food processor.

Lightly sauté the onions in a little butter. Let cool, then purée and add to the vegetables.

In a small pan, bring one-third of the milk almost to a boil. Melt the remaining butter in a large heavy pan. Add the flour to the butter and cook 3 minutes over medium heat. Add the nutmeg and pepper. Stirring constantly, pour in the hot milk, then add the vegetable purée. Still stirring, bring gently to a boil, then simmer 5 minutes.

Add 2 cups of the reserved stock and return to the blender or food processor for a final puréeing.

Return the soup to a saucepan. Add the remaining milk and the cream and heat through, but do not let boil. Adjust the seasoning, if necessary.

While the soup is heating, make the rouille: Soak the bread in water to soften, then squeeze dry. Put the soaked bread in a blender or food processor together with the egg yolk, garlic, red peppers, cayenne, and saffron. Blend thoroughly and then add the oil and 2 tablespoons of the reserved stock, with the blender still running. Season.

To serve, pour the soup into warmed bowls and place 2 teaspoons of rouille in the center of each.

GOLDEN SWEDISH SOUP

SERVES 4–6

1¾ cups yellow split peas
2 tsp salt
4 tbsp butter
2 large onions, diced
½ tsp ground ginger
2½ cups milk
2 chicken bouillon cubes
freshly ground black pepper

Soak the peas overnight. Rinse and place in a pan of fresh cold water. Bring slowly to a boil. Drain, rinse, and place in 1¾ quarts of fresh cold water. Bring to a boil again, then simmer until tender 40–60 minutes, adding the salt halfway through. Drain off the water.

Melt the butter in a heavy pan, then add the onions and ginger. Sauté until the onions are just translucent. Add to the pan of split peas.

Place the milk in a small pan and heat gently. Add the chicken bouillon cubes and stir until completely dissolved. Let cool, then add to the split peas.

Purée the soup in a blender or food processor. If too thick, add a little more milk or water. Reheat and season with pepper before serving.

CHILLED SORREL SOUP WITH SEAFOOD★

SERVES 8–10

2 tbsp salt
1 lb sorrel
2 tbsp sugar
2 tbsp lemon juice
3 eggs, beaten
(★see page 2 for advice on eggs)
2 tbsp milk
1 large cucumber, peeled and diced
½ lb chilled mixed cooked seafood, such as peeled
shrimp, young mussels, bay scallops
1 cup sour cream
2 tbsp minced scallions (including the green tops)

Put 2¼ quarts of water with the salt in a large pan over medium heat.

Remove any large ribs from the sorrel, wash, and shake the leaves. Place them on top of each other. Roll into a fat cigar shape and slice it across thinly.

Add the shredded sorrel to the water and bring it to a boil. Reduce the heat to low and simmer 30 minutes. Add the sugar and lemon juice and cook 15 minutes longer.

Put the eggs in a bowl together with the milk. Pour 1 cup of the hot sorrel stock over the eggs in a steady stream, stirring. Pour the egg mixture back into the soup pan, still stirring. Remove the pan from the heat and let cool completely. Season and chill at least 2 hours or, preferably, overnight.

Arrange the diced cucumber in the bottom of the serving bowls. Add the soup, followed by the seafood and sour cream. Sprinkle with scallions and serve.

HERB SOUP WITH CHEESE CROUTONS

SERVES 4–6

2 tbsp butter
1 onion, finely grated
3 stalks of celery, minced
½ tsp celery salt
1 tbsp each of minced fresh parsley, chervil, tarragon,
and chives
3 tbsp dry white wine
3½ cups vegetable stock
freshly ground black pepper
FOR THE CROUTONS
4 slices of whole wheat bread, crusts removed
4 tbsp butter
½ cup grated cheese, such as Cheddar or Swiss
1 small garlic clove, minced

Melt the butter in a heavy pan over medium heat. Add the onion, celery, and celery salt. Sauté gently 3 minutes.

Add the herbs and white wine. Cover and let simmer 5 minutes, then add the stock. Bring gently to a boil, then cover and simmer 5 minutes longer.

While the soup is simmering, make the croutons: Spread the slices of bread lightly with some of the butter. Cover them with grated cheese, sandwich them in 2 pairs, and press down firmly. Slice these sandwiches into tiny cubes.

Melt the remaining butter in a sauté pan over medium heat. Add the garlic and sauté gently until it begins to brown. Toss the bread cubes in the butter and garlic until they are well browned on all sides.

Season the soup with black pepper, pour it into warmed bowls, and scatter some of the croutons over the top of each.

CROUTONS of bread fried in butter can be flavored in many other ways, such as with fresh herbs or cayenne pepper. Other decorative and tasty finishes for soups include chopped hard-cooked egg, celery shreds, quenelles of white fish, or minced shrimp.

When cooking dried beans it is important to discard the water in which they are first boiled and to replace this with fresh water for the remaining cooking as this removes any toxins. Beans should be brought to a boil slowly and cooked fairly gently to prevent splitting. Salt should only be added later in the cooking, as it hardens the beans.

CREAM OF BLACK-EYED PEA SOUP

SERVES 6–8

2 ⅓ cups black-eyed peas, soaked overnight in cold water
6 tbsp butter
3 onions, chopped
¾ cup chopped carrots
¾ cup chopped celery
2 garlic cloves, minced
1 ½ quarts vegetable stock
bouquet garni
1 tsp lemon juice
salt and freshly ground black pepper
1 cup light cream
1–2 tbsp cranberry sauce
1 tbsp minced fresh parsley, for garnish

Drain the peas, put them in a pan, and cover with fresh cold water. Bring to a boil, drain, and cover again with fresh water. Bring to a boil once more, cover, and simmer until tender, about 40 minutes.

Melt the butter in a frying pan over medium-low heat. Add the onions, carrots, celery, and garlic and sauté 10 minutes. Transfer the vegetables to a large pan and add the vegetable stock, cooked peas, and the bouquet garni. Bring to a boil, cover, and simmer 20 minutes.

Discard the bouquet garni. Add the lemon juice and season the soup to taste. Let cool.

When cool, purée the soup in a blender or food processor. Stir in the cream, then heat through, being careful not to let it boil.

Ladle the soup into 6–8 warmed bowls and spoon some of the cranberry sauce in the center of each. Garnish with parsley and serve.

Chilled Lettuce Soup

CHILLED LETTUCE SOUP

SERVES 4

1 large head of butterhead lettuce
3 tbsp butter
6 fat scallions, chopped (including green tops)
1 large purple garlic clove, minced
3 potatoes, diced
1 quart vegetable stock or 2 vegetable bouillon cubes dissolved in 1 quart spring water
3 tbsp light cream
1 tbsp chopped fresh parsley
1 tsp coarse salt
freshly ground black pepper
ice cubes, for serving

Separate the lettuce leaves and tear them into bits.

Melt the butter in a large heavy pan over medium heat. Toss in the lettuce leaves, scallions, and garlic. Sauté lightly 5 minutes.

Add the potatoes and the vegetable stock and simmer until the potatoes are tender, about 45 minutes. Let cool and then chill 2 hours.

Just before serving, stir in the cream and parsley. Season and add a large ice cube to each portion.

As in FIVE-BEAN SOUP WITH GARLIC AND GOOSEBERRY, *an alternative to spooning swirls of cream decoratively into soups before serving is to add fruit and vegetable purées with complementary colors and flavors. Try avocado purée in tomato soup, tomato purée in spinach soup, and applesauce in pea and ham soup.*

CHILLED BEET AND HORSERADISH SOUP

SERVES 6–8

6 raw beets (see below)
1 ½ quarts chicken stock
8 scallions (including green tops), chopped
½ cucumber, peeled, halved lengthwise, and seeded
juice of ½ lime
1 tsp dark brown sugar
2 tsp freshly grated horseradish root
⅔ cup light cream
salt and freshly ground black pepper
6–8 tbsp sour cream
2 large dill pickles, thinly sliced, for garnish
½ tbsp minced fresh dill leaves, for garnish

Try to buy beets that still have their stems and leaves and an intact skin. It is also a good idea to buy ones of a uniform size so that they will cook in the same time.

Put the stock in a large pan and bring to a boil. Place the beets gently in the stock, cover, and simmer until they are completely tender, 15–20 minutes.

Trying to avoid breaking the skins, remove the beets from the stock. Let cool completely and reserve the stock.

Once cool, peel and coarsely dice the beets and leaves. Purée in a blender or food processor, together with the scallions and cucumber.

Mix with the reserved stock, lime juice, sugar, horseradish, and light cream. Chill at least 3 hours.

To serve: Adjust the seasoning and pour the chilled soup into bowls. Place a spoonful of sour cream in the middle of each bowl, then garnish with the slices of pickle and some minced dill leaves.

FIVE-BEAN SOUP WITH GARLIC AND GOOSEBERRY

SERVES 6

3 tbsp butter
1 tbsp olive oil
3 garlic cloves, sliced
1 large onion, sliced
2 leeks, cut into ½-inch slices
3 ½ cups vegetable stock
½ lb potatoes, cut into small chunks
1 ½ cups fresh gooseberries, halved
3 cups mixed cooked beans: kidney, flageolet, lima, navy, and black-eyed pea
salt and freshly ground black pepper

Melt the butter with the oil in a large heavy pan over low heat. Add the garlic and cook gently 3 minutes, stirring constantly. Add the onion and leeks and sauté 5 minutes.

Add the stock and bring to a boil. Reduce the heat, add the potatoes, and simmer until they are tender, 15–20 minutes.

Place the gooseberries in a small pan with a few spoonfuls of water and bring to a boil. Simmer until they are reduced to a pulp. Remove from the heat, let cool a little, and then push them through a strainer to make a coulis.

Add the cooked beans to the potato and vegetable broth. Heat through but do not bring to a boil.

Season and pour into warmed soup bowls. Drizzle some of the gooseberry coulis into each and serve immediately.

Left: Five-Bean Soup with Garlic and Gooseberry; right: Chilled Beet and Horseradish Soup

BEEFSTEAK TOMATO AND OKRA SOUP

SERVES 4

4 tbsp butter
6 scallions (including the green tops), sliced
½ lb okra, sliced
1 garlic clove, minced
3 large beefsteak tomatoes, peeled, seeded, and sliced
1 tbsp light brown sugar
1 tsp soy sauce
3 ½ cups vegetable stock
1 tsp grated zest and 1 tbsp juice from a washed lemon
1 heaped tbsp chopped fresh cilantro, for garnish
salt and freshly ground black pepper

Melt the butter in a heavy pan over medium heat. Add the scallions, okra, garlic, and tomatoes and sauté gently 7 minutes. Add the remaining ingredients, cover, and simmer 10 minutes.

Season, and add the coriander just before serving.

PETITPOIS AND LEMONGRASS SOUP

SERVES 4

2 stalks of lemongrass
3 ½ cups vegetable stock
4 tbsp butter
1 large onion, diced
2 large potatoes, diced
¾ lb (2 ⅓ cups) frozen small green peas, thawed
salt and freshly ground black pepper

Using a rolling pin, crush the bulbous part of the lemongrass stalks and place them in a pan. Add one-third of the stock. Cover, bring just to a simmer, and cook over very low heat 30 minutes.

Meanwhile, melt the butter in a large pan over medium heat and toss the onion and potatoes 5 minutes. Add the remaining stock and bring to boil. Cover and simmer 30 minutes.

Remove the pan with the lemongrass from the heat. Discard the lemongrass, then add the peas. Let them sit 15 minutes, off the heat.

Add the contents of this pan to the other. Season and let cool, then purée in a blender or food processor. Reheat the soup gently for serving.

LENTIL SOUP WITH FRESH GINGER

SERVES 4

1 ¼ cups lentils, soaked overnight
1 large onion, diced
1 large purple garlic clove, minced
2 tbsp corn or canola oil
1 ¼ cups vegetable stock
1 ¼ cups low-fat milk
1 oz peeled fresh gingerroot, grated
salt and freshly ground black pepper
⅓ cup sesame seeds, toasted
1 tbsp chopped fresh parsley, for garnish

Drain the lentils thoroughly, then bring them to a boil in 2 cups of water over medium heat. Simmer until tender, 20–30 minutes.

In a large heavy pan, sauté the onion and garlic in the oil until translucent. Add the vegetable stock and milk. Bring to a boil and simmer 10 minutes. Add the lentils with their stock and the ginger. Season, then simmer 15 minutes longer. Let cool, then purée in a blender or food processor.

Reheat for serving, being careful not to let it boil. Put some of the sesame seeds in the bottom of each of the warmed serving bowls, reserving some for garnish. Fill the bowls with soup and garnish with the remaining sesame seeds and the parsley.

LEEK AND POTATO SOUP

SERVES 6–8

4 tbsp butter
2 lb leeks, sliced into ¼-inch pieces
1 lb thin-skinned potatoes (preferably red), unpeeled
and coarsely diced
2 large stalks of celery, chopped
2½ cups chicken stock
2½ cups low-fat milk
½ tsp freshly grated nutmeg
salt and freshly ground black pepper
1¼ cups whipping cream
minced fresh parsley, for garnish

Melt the butter in a large heavy pan over medium heat. Add the leeks and potatoes and cook gently 7–10 minutes, stirring constantly.

Add the celery. Stir in the stock and milk and bring to a boil. Add the nutmeg and season with salt and pepper. Reduce the heat and simmer 30 minutes.

If serving cold, let cool completely and then purée in a blender or food processor. Stir in the cream and chill at least 2 hours. Adjust the seasoning, if necessary, and serve garnished with parsley.

If serving hot, stir in the cream and warm through gently, without letting it boil. Adjust the seasoning, if necessary, pour into warmed bowls, and garnish with the parsley.

Note: For a hot smooth soup, let the mixture cool before blending and then reheat.

ROQUEFORT AND SAVOY CABBAGE SOUP

SERVES 6–8

½ lb Canadian bacon, cut into strips
10 whole cloves
2 onions, quartered
3 leeks, chopped
4 carrots, chopped
1 large head of Savoy cabbage
4 potatoes, diced
6–8 slices of whole wheat bread, lightly toasted
½ lb Roquefort cheese
salt and freshly ground black pepper

Put 2 quarts of cold water in a pan and place over medium heat. Add the bacon and bring to a boil. Skim, then simmer 15 minutes. Skim again.

Stick the cloves into the onion quarters, and add these to the stock together with the leeks and carrots. Simmer 30 minutes longer.

Quarter the cabbage, cutting out the core and any thick ribs on outer leaves. Blanch 3 minutes in a large pan of boiling water. Drain and refresh under cold running water, then cut into strips.

Add the cabbage strips to the stock and cook 20 minutes over moderate heat. Add the potatoes and simmer 30 minutes or so longer, until they are tender. Remove the cloves, if preferred.

Place a slice of toast in the bottom of each of the warmed bowls and crumble the cheese over it.

Season the soup with pepper (no salt should be necessary due to the high salt content of the cheese), pour it into the bowls, and serve.

Other blue cheeses, such as Gorgonzola, Stilton, or Danish Blue, can be substituted for Roquefort in this soup, but the flavor will not be quite the same.

APPETIZERS AND HORS D'ŒUVRES

Appetizers and hors d'œuvres should stimulate the appetite for the rest of the meal by both tickling the tastebuds and appealing to the eye. For this reason, interesting and unusual combinations of ingredients and inviting presentation are the most important factors in a successful first course. Appetizers are also useful elements in the construction of balanced meals, for instance providing a salad of raw vegetables before a heavy main course. Many appetizers can also easily be scaled up to become substantial main courses, or they can be served just as they are as light meals, possibly with good crusty bread and/or an accompanying salad. By their nature, appetizers and hors d'œuvres also make good party food, and a combination of several such dishes, served as bite-sized finger-food, can make an impressive, satisfying, and healthy buffet spread.

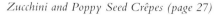

Zucchini and Poppy Seed Crêpes (page 27)

Instead of cutting the vegetables into julienne strips, try grating them on a mandoline grater for ease, speed, and finer results.

VEGETABLE JULIENNE WITH COCONUT-LIME DRESSING

SERVES 4–6

¼ lb each carrots, fennel, cucumber, celeriac, and
zucchini, cut into julienne strips
¼ lb firm broccoli florets, cut into small pieces
FOR THE COCONUT-LIME DRESSING
⅔ cup Basic Vinaigrette (see page 12), made using
Japanese rice vinegar instead of wine vinegar
1 tbsp coconut cream
½ tsp finely grated zest from a washed lime
salt and freshly ground black pepper

Place all the vegetables in a wire basket and plunge them into rapidly boiling salted water to blanch 1 minute.

Test for texture: If still not quite tender enough, blanch 1 minute longer. Drain and refresh under cold running water.

Make the coconut-lime dressing by stirring the additional ingredients into the vinaigrette and adjusting the seasoning, if necessary.

Serve the vegetable julienne hot, warm, or cold, tossed in the dressing while still warm.

MUSHROOMS WITH ORANGE AND CILANTRO

SERVES 4

2 tbsp butter
1 tbsp olive oil
¾ lb open mushrooms, coarsely chopped
¼ cup cider vinegar
1 vegetable bouillon cube
1 tsp finely grated zest and the juice from ½ large
washed orange
salt and freshly ground black pepper
1 tbsp minced fresh cilantro leaves
½ 4-oz jar pimientos, drained and diced
sesame crackers or hot toast, for serving

Melt the butter with the oil in a heavy pan over medium heat. Add the mushrooms and toss so that they are well coated. Add the cider vinegar and then reduce the heat. Let simmer gently 5 minutes, stirring from time to time.

Crumble the vegetable bouillon cube over the mushrooms, then add the orange juice. Cook, stirring frequently, 5 minutes longer.

Add the orange zest and season with pepper and a very little salt, if necessary (the bouillon cube will probably have a high salt content). Boil the liquid to reduce it to a smooth sauce. Remove from the heat and let cool.

Mix in the cilantro and pimiento thoroughly. Turn the mixture into a bowl, cover, and chill 1 hour.

Serve with sesame crackers or hot toast.

ZUCCHINI AND POPPY SEED CRÊPES

MAKES 8

1 ¼ cups flour
pinch of salt
½ tbsp poppy seeds
grated zest of a washed lemon
freshly ground black pepper
2 eggs
2 cups milk
2 tbsp butter, melted
2 tbsp finely shredded zucchini

In a large bowl, mix the flour, salt, poppy seeds, and lemon zest with some pepper. Make a well in the center and break in the eggs. Add half the milk and work these liquid ingredients into the flour.

Add half the melted butter to the remaining milk, then mix this into the flour mixture. When well mixed, stir in the shredded zucchini.

Cook the crêpes in a heavy 7-inch frying pan: Heat a little of the remaining butter in the pan over medium-high heat. When very hot, but not burning, pour in just enough batter to cover the bottom of the pan thinly. Cook until the batter bubbles, then flip and cook until golden on both sides.

Note: For a more substantial dish, roll the crêpes around a filling. Try any of the following: cheese, such as Cheddar or freshly grated Parmesan; cooked vegetables, such as spinach, onions, or carrots; or sauces, such as cheese or fresh tomato.

BAKED TAPENADE TOASTS

SERVES 4

1 large head of garlic
1 ½ oz anchovy fillets in oil, drained
2 tbsp capers in vinegar, drained
1 ⅓ cups large black olives, pitted
1 tbsp extra virgin olive oil
freshly ground black pepper
8 thin slices of whole wheat toast

Preheat the oven to 400°F.

Place the whole garlic head on a baking sheet and bake 30 minutes. Remove from the oven, let cool slightly, and then squeeze the cloves out of their skins.

Put the garlic cloves in a blender or food processor, together with the anchovies, capers, olives, and the olive oil. Season with black pepper and blend 2 minutes.

Spread this mixture generously on the toast, then cut it into large bite-size squares and serve immediately.

TOASTS *lend themselves to endless variations. Try spreading them with a mixture of coarsely chopped shrimp mixed with lime zest and butter, or ground chicken blended with chestnut purée.*

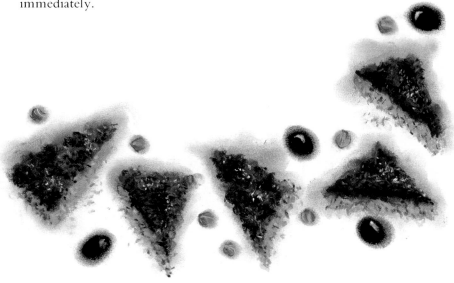

CUCUMBER AND SHRIMP MOUSSE WITH MANDARINS

SERVES 4

1 large cucumber, peeled and thinly sliced
3 tbsp whipping cream
1 cup ricotta cheese
1 cup low-fat cream cheese
2 envelopes unflavored gelatin
½ cup canned mandarin oranges in their own juice
4 large scallions (including green tops), minced
¼ lb peeled cooked small shrimp
½ tsp grated zest and ½ tsp juice from a washed lime
½ tsp lemon juice
½ tsp each minced fresh dill, chives, and parsley
salt and freshly ground black pepper
3 cooked shrimp in shell, for garnish (optional)

If you want a particularly low-fat mousse, use part-skim ricotta. It has less than 10% fat.

Place the cucumber slices in a colander, sprinkle with salt, and let them drain, with a heavy plate on top, for 1½ hours. Rinse and pat dry.

In a large bowl, whip the cream until just stiff and then add the cheeses. Season to taste.

In another large bowl, dissolve the gelatin in the warmed juice from the mandarins. Add the remaining ingredients, mixing gently together to blend in the gelatin. Add this to the cream and cheese mixture, reserving some mandarins and shrimp to place in the bottom of the mold. Season the mixture.

Line a 4-cup mold with the cucumber slices and add any left to the cheese mixture. Arrange the reserved mandarins and shrimp in the bottom of the mold and then pour in the mixture. Chill overnight.

Unmold for serving and garnish with shrimp in shell, if using.

Left and right: Sorrel and Tomato Mousse (page 30) made in individual ramekins; center: Cucumber and Shrimp Mousse with Mandarins

AGAR-AGAR *is a jelling agent widely used in Japanese cooking and Western commercial food manufacture. It is a good alternative to gelatin as, being made from seaweed, it can be eaten by vegetarians and is full of healthy minerals.*

SORREL AND TOMATO MOUSSE

SERVES 4

10 oz sorrel, stems and thick ribs removed
3 tbsp butter
2 ½ cups gelatinous meat stock, melted
salt and freshly ground black pepper
1 ¼ cups whipping cream, whipped to soft peaks
1 large onion, minced
⅓ cup dry white wine
1 ¼ lb ripe beefsteak tomatoes, seeded and coarsely chopped
½ tsp chopped fresh basil
½ tsp brown sugar

Reserving some small leaves for garnish, sauté the sorrel in two-thirds of the butter over low heat 20 minutes, stirring constantly, until almost dry.

Add ⅔ cup of the meat stock and boil to reduce the mixture by half, stirring all the time. (It should now resemble a semi-liquid purée.)

Season, then press through a fine sieve into a glass bowl. Stir in 5 tablespoons more of the remaining stock.

Set this bowl in a larger dish and surround with crushed ice. Stir the mousse until it begins to thicken. Stir in half the cream and check the seasoning again. Set aside in the bowl of ice.

Melt the remaining butter in a heavy pan over medium heat and lightly sauté the onion 15 minutes. Add the wine, raise the heat to high, and, stirring constantly, boil to reduce the liquid until the pan is almost dry.

Add the tomatoes, basil, and sugar. Simmer, uncovered, 30 minutes, stirring several times.

Add ½ cup of the remaining stock and boil to reduce the mixture by about half, stirring constantly.

Season and press the mixture through a fine sieve into a bowl. Stir in another ½ cup of the remaining stock and mix well.

Set this bowl in a dish surrounded by crushed ice and follow the same procedure as for the sorrel mousse. Just before it sets, stir and fold in the cream. Adjust the seasoning, if necessary.

Spoon the tomato mousse over the sorrel mousse, cover, and chill 2 hours longer.

Warm the remaining meat stock again until just liquid and let it cool to room temperature. Pour this over the two mousses and then chill overnight.

Serve the mousse spooned from the glass bowl, garnished with the reserved sorrel leaves.

Note: This mousse can be made in individual ramekins. Set the ramekins on a bed of ice and pour in each mousse after the cream has been added.

BROCCOLI WITH RADISHES AND TAHINI

SERVES 4

½ lb broccoli florets
3 large, long pink radishes, thinly sliced
½ tbsp tahini paste
½ tbsp light soy sauce
juice of ½ lime
1 garlic clove

Bring a pan of water to a boil, plunge in the broccoli florets, and blanch until tender, but still crunchy, 2–3 minutes. Immediately drain well and place in a warmed serving dish. Sprinkle the radish slices over the broccoli and keep warm.

Put the remaining ingredients in a blender or food processor together with 1 tablespoon of water. Process 1 minute.

Pour this dressing over the vegetables and serve.

FINE GREEN BEANS WITH GINGER AND ALMONDS

SERVES 4

1 ½ lb fine green beans
1 oz agar-agar flakes
1 ¾ quarts pear juice
6 tbsp barley malt syrup
pinch of sea salt
2 tbsp juice from freshly grated gingerroot
1 cup almonds, toasted

Steam the beans until just tender, 7–10 minutes. Drain and set aside.

In a pan, soak the agar-agar in the pear juice 15 minutes. Then bring to a boil. Reduce the heat, add the malt syrup and the salt, and stir until the flakes have dissolved. Add the ginger juice.

Rinse a shallow dish and pour in the juice mixture. Let cool until almost set. Stir vigorously and chill until just setting. Stir in the almonds. Put most of the beans in a serving dish and spoon the jelled mixture on top. Chill 30 minutes longer before serving, garnished with the remaining beans.

LEEKS VINAIGRETTE

SERVES 4

4 young leeks, trimmed and cut in half lengthwise
⅔ cup Basic Vinaigrette (see page 12)

Place the leeks in a pan that has a tight-fitting lid. Add 6 tablespoons of water, cover, and steam, about 15 minutes. Drain and let cool.

Arrange in a serving dish, pour over vinaigrette, and let marinate in the refrigerator about 2 hours.

Top: Leeks Vinaigrette garnished with blanched orange zest; bottom: Broccoli with Radishes and Tahini

MAIN COURSES

Fortunately, the old concept of 'meat and potatoes' main courses is now dying away at all levels. As well as the pressure of more and more families now having at least one vegetarian in their ranks, greater foreign travel – with a resulting awareness of other cuisines – and the extraordinary range of fresh vegetables, salad greens, herbs, and fruit now available in our markets has caused even the most conventional cooks to broaden their horizons. Cultures that have traditionally made more of vegetables – or perhaps used meat and fish primarily as flavoring ingredients – include the Mediterranean peoples, the Indians, Chinese, Japanese, and Latin Americans. Looking toward their heritage gives us a myriad of wonderful ways to prepare substantial main-course salads and other dishes based mainly on vegetables.

Left: Spuds Supreme (page 34); right:
Grandmother's Potato Pancakes (page 34)

GRANDMOTHER'S POTATO PANCAKES

SERVES 4

1 ½ lb freshly cooked potatoes
1 tbsp butter
1 egg yolk
2 tbsp whipping cream
1 tsp salt
½ tsp freshly grated nutmeg
freshly ground black pepper
6 tbsp whole wheat bread crumbs
2 tbsp corn oil

Mash the potatoes well, then mix in the butter, egg yolk, cream, salt, nutmeg, and pepper to taste.

Divide the mixture into 8 equal portions and shape into fat cakes. Then roll the cakes in bread crumbs to coat the outsides evenly.

Put the oil in a frying pan over medium heat and fry the cakes until golden brown on both sides.

Drain briefly on paper towels and serve with apple sauce if desired.

SPUDS SUPREME

SERVES 6

6 large baking potatoes
¼ cup garlic-flavored soft cream cheese
⅓ cup canned tuna in oil, drained
freshly ground black pepper
about 2 tbsp olive oil
about ¼ cup coarse salt

Preheat the oven to 400°F.

Using an apple corer, take a cylinder from the middle of each potato.

Mix the cheese and the tuna well together. Season with pepper and use to fill the cavities in the potatoes, plugging both ends with a small cut-off section of the removed cylinder. Coat the potatoes with oil, then sprinkle them with coarse salt.

Place the potatoes on a baking sheet in the middle of the oven and bake until tender, about 1 hour. Serve accompanied by any remaining stuffing.

Note: Any cheese can be used for this dish, or even a combination of cheese and minced vegetables, such as onion, carrot, celery, etc.

MIXED WILD MUSHROOM CASSEROLE

SERVES 4

2 tbsp sunflower or canola oil
2 tbsp hazelnut oil
2 onions, diced
2 large purple garlic cloves, chopped
½ tsp crushed coriander seeds
½ tsp herbes de Provence
2 stalks of celery, chopped
3 zucchini, sliced
3 large beefsteak tomatoes, seeded and coarsely chopped
salt and freshly ground black pepper
1 ½ lb mixed wild mushrooms (oyster, chanterelle, porcini, etc.)
⅓ cup dry red wine
⅔ cup crème fraîche or whipping cream

Put the oils in a flameproof casserole dish over medium heat. Add the onions, garlic, coriander, and herbs. Sauté 3 minutes.

Add the celery and zucchini and sauté 3 minutes longer. Then add the tomatoes, stirring to mix them in thoroughly. Season. Add the mushrooms and red wine. Stir 3 minutes. Reduce the heat, cover, and simmer gently 15 minutes.

Remove from the heat and stir in the cream. Adjust the seasoning, if necessary, before serving.

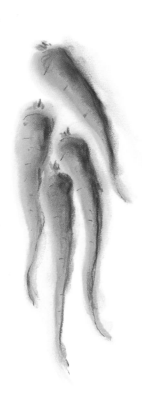

WILD MUSHROOMS *are increasingly seen in gourmet food stores. If none are available, try to get some shiitake and/or oyster mushrooms.*

POTATOES WITH WINTER VEGETABLE TRICOLOR

SERVES 4

1 lb thin-skinned potatoes, washed but not peeled
½ tbsp coarse salt
1 large head of celeriac, peeled and cut into chunks
1½ lb spinach, stems removed
3 large carrots, thinly sliced
salt and freshly ground black pepper
½ tsp celery salt
1 tbsp light cream
¼ tsp freshly grated nutmeg

Put the potatoes and coarse salt in a pan of water and place over medium heat. Bring to a boil, reduce the heat, and cook the potatoes until tender. Drain and place them on a warm plate. The salt should dry on the potato skins.

When cool enough to handle, cut the potatoes into thick slices. Keep warm.

Preheat the oven to 450°F.

Cook the celeriac in unsalted boiling water until tender, 15–20 minutes. Steam the spinach until tender, 10–15 minutes. Cook the carrots in the celeriac water until tender, 15–20 minutes.

Blend each vegetable individually to a purée. Season the purées and add the celery salt to the celery root, the cream to the spinach, and the nutmeg to the carrots.

Spoon the purées decoratively over the potatoes. Place them in the oven and heat through 5 minutes. Serve immediately.

VEGETABLE BOUCHÉES

MAKES 12–14

1 lb puff pastry
1 egg, beaten
2 tbsp butter
1½–2 cups diced mixed vegetables, such as carrot, onion, zucchini, celeriac and broccoli
1¼ cups Béchamel Sauce (see page 10)
salt and freshly ground black pepper

Preheat the oven to 450°F.

Roll out the pastry to a thickness of about ¼ inch. Using a 2-inch round cutter, cut out as many disks as possible. Press a 1-inch round cutter into the center of each disk without going all the way through, to make the bouchée "lids."

Brush the pastry disks with beaten eggs, arrange on a baking sheet, and bake 15 minutes.

Toward the end of this time, melt the butter in a sauté pan over medium heat and lightly sauté the vegetables 3–5 minutes. In a large bowl, mix the vegetables with the sauce and adjust the seasoning.

Remove the sheet of cooked bouchées from the oven and carefully pry out the central "lids" with the tip of a sharp knife. Spoon the filling into the cases and return to the oven to warm through 5 minutes.

Remove and place on a warmed serving platter. Put the pastry "lids" back in place and serve immediately.

Note: For alternative fillings, try using only 1½ cups of the diced mixed vegetables and adding to them ¼–½ cup of diced ham, cooked chicken, tuna, or smoked fish.

The even more adventurous might like to place an additional spoonful or two of béchamel sauce mixed with some chopped capers in the bouchées and then nest a soft-cooked quail egg in each.

HERBES DE PROVENCE *consist of mixed bay, thyme, rosemary, basil, and savory, usually dried. Ready-made mixtures are available in gourmet stores and some supermarkets.*

CURLY ENDIVE LOAF WITH CAPER SAUCE

SERVES 4

5 heads of curly endive
5 tbsp butter
¼ cup flour
1 cup cream
4 eggs, beaten
salt and freshly ground black pepper
FOR THE CAPER SAUCE
2 tbsp butter
2 tbsp olive oil
2 onions, sliced
¾ lb tomatoes, peeled, seeded, and coarsely chopped
1 ½ tbsp capers

Preheat the oven to 350°F.

Put 3½ quarts of water in a large pan and bring it to a boil. Carefully place the endive heads in the water, bring it back to a boil, and cook, uncovered, 15 minutes. Drain and let cool. Then squeeze out all remaining liquid and chop the endive coarsely.

Make a béchamel sauce (see page 10), using 4 tablespoons of the butter, the flour, and cream. Add the beaten eggs and then the chopped endive. Season.

Grease a 1-quart charlotte mold with the remaining butter. Fill with the mixture, tapping the mold sharply from time to time to remove air pockets. Let settle.

Place the mold in 2 inches of hot water in a deep roasting pan. Put this in the oven and bake until the surface of the loaf is golden brown, about 1 hour. The water should not boil at any time during the baking.

While the loaf is cooking, make the caper sauce: Melt the butter with the oil in a heavy pan over medium heat. Add the onions and sauté until translucent. Then add the tomatoes and cook until tender, about 5–7 minutes. Season and let cool slightly. Then purée in a blender or food processor and stir in the capers.

Remove the loaf from oven. Insert a knife to the bottom of the mold: If it comes out clean the loaf is cooked through; if sticky, return it to the oven for a further 10–15 minutes baking.

Let cool out of the oven 3 minutes and then unmold on a warmed serving dish and serve with the caper sauce.

LEEK, MOZZARELLA, AND PESTO GRATIN

SERVES 4

8 large leeks, trimmed but leaving as much green as
possible
½ cup low-fat cream cheese
2 tbsp pesto sauce
¼ cup pine nuts
¼ lb mozzarella cheese, thinly sliced
salt and freshly ground black pepper

Preheat the oven to 400°F.

Cut each of the leeks into 4 equal lengths. Place them in a pan of boiling salted water and cook 5–7 minutes. Remove, refresh under cold running water, and place in colander to drain.

Place the drained leeks in an ovenproof dish. Mix the cream cheese and pesto together and season. Using a spatula, smooth the mixture over the leeks. Sprinkle over the pine nuts and arrange the mozzarella slices over the top.

Bake 20–30 minutes, until the mozzarella has turned golden brown.

Left to right: Leek, Mozzarella, and Pesto Gratin; Japanese Pickled Vegetables (page 58); Vegetable Bouchées (page 35)

TOFU, or bean curd, is made from soybeans and is rich in proteins. Rather like fresh cheese in appearance and texture, its gentle flavor lends its use with a variety of vegetables, herbs, and spices. It is particularly tasty when smoked.

PUMPKIN STUFFED WITH LEEKS AND SMOKED TOFU

SERVES 2

1 pumpkin, weighing 2–3 lb
1 ½ tbsp light soy sauce
2 tsp Asian sesame oil
½ lb smoked tofu, mashed
2 young leeks, thinly sliced or shredded
½ tsp freshly grated nutmeg

Preheat the oven to 400°F.

Cut off the top of the pumpkin and reserve. Scoop out and discard all the seeds and fibers.

Mix the soy sauce and oil into the tofu with the leeks and nutmeg. Pack the mixture into the pumpkin and place the top back on. Wrap in foil and bake 1–1½ hours, depending on size.

Remove the top and halve the pumpkin to serve.

CAULIFLOWER CHEESE CASSEROLE WITH NUTS AND OATS

SERVES 4–6

1 large head of cauliflower
4 tbsp unsalted butter
2 onions, minced
1 ¼ cups milk
¾ cup shredded Swiss cheese
salt and freshly ground black pepper
5 eggs, beaten
2 cups fresh whole wheat bread crumbs
3 tbsp almonds, toasted
3 tbsp hazelnuts, toasted
1 cup rolled oats

Preheat the oven to 350°F.

Remove all large outer leaves surrounding the cauliflower, but leave the young green ones. Cut the cauliflower lengthwise into 6 parts, complete with core.

Place the cauliflower in a large pan of lightly salted water. Bring to a boil, then reduce the heat and simmer 5 minutes. Drain thoroughly and place in a 2-quart ovenproof dish.

Melt half the butter in a sauté pan over medium heat and sauté the onions until soft.

Bring the milk to a boil in a saucepan and stir in the Swiss cheese and the remaining butter. Season with salt and pepper and stir in the onions. Remove from the heat, then blend in the eggs and one-third of the bread crumbs. Cover the drained cauliflower with this sauce and bake on the middle shelf of the oven for 20 minutes.

Remove the baking dish from the oven and sprinkle with the nuts, oats, and remaining bread crumbs. Return to the oven, turn the heat up to 400°F and bake until the oats are golden, 10–15 minutes.

RATATOUILLE

SERVES 4

6 zucchini
6 eggplants
2 green sweet peppers
2 red sweet peppers
2¼ cups extra virgin olive oil
4 large onions, each cut into 6 pieces
6 tomatoes, peeled, seeded, and coarsely chopped
4 purple garlic cloves, minced
large sprig of fresh oregano
juice of ½ large lemon
salt and freshly ground black pepper

Cut the zucchini and eggplants into slices about ¾-inch thick. Arrange these on a wire rack and sprinkle generously with salt. Let drain 30 minutes, then rinse and pat dry with paper towel.

While these drain, skin the peppers by piercing them with a fork and holding them over a flame or under the broiler. Turn them so that the skin blisters uniformly. Let cool slightly; the blackened skin will come off with ease. Cut the peppers in half, remove the seeds, and slice the flesh in thick strips.

Pour 7 tablespoons of the oil into a large frying pan over medium heat, then add the zucchini. Raise the heat and cook until the slices are browned on both sides. Using a slotted spoon, transfer the zucchini to a large flameproof casserole. Repeat this process with the eggplant, onions, and peppers, adding more oil as necessary.

Add tomatoes, garlic, oregano, and rest of the oil to the casserole. Add lemon juice and season with pepper but no salt. Place over medium heat and cover. Bring to a boil, then lower heat and simmer gently 50–60 minutes, stirring once or twice.

Season with salt. (If there is surplus liquid, drain it off into a pan and boil rapidly to reduce it; then return it to the dish.) Serve hot, warm, or cold.

DEEP-FRIED EGGPLANT WITH BLACK BEAN SAUCE

SERVES 4

6 small to medium eggplants
2 eggs, beaten
3 tbsp flour
salt and freshly ground black pepper
2 tbsp black bean sauce
vegetable or peanut oil, for deep-frying

Cut the eggplants across into disks about ¾-inch thick. Lay these flat, sprinkle with salt, and let drain 30 minutes. Rinse and pat dry.

Put the egg in a small bowl and put the flour on a shallow plate. Season the flour.

Spread both sides of each eggplant slice with a thin coating of black bean sauce. Dip both sides of each slice into the beaten egg, then in the flour. Shake off any excess flour.

Place a batch of eggplant slices in a single layer in the wire basket of a deep-fryer. Heat the oil in the deep-fryer to 360°F (a small cube of dry bread browns in 60 seconds). Fry the eggplant until well browned, 2–3 minutes.

Drain on paper towels, then place on a warmed serving dish. Serve as soon as all the slices are fried.

Bottled or canned BLACK BEAN SAUCE *is now readily available in Asian groceries and supermarkets. It will give an authentic Cantonese flavor to many foods, especially stir-fry dishes.*

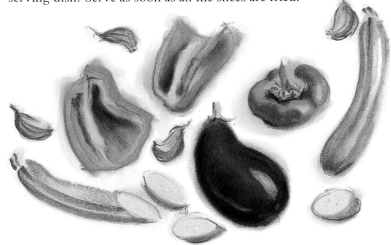

RED LENTILS WITH CINNAMON AND COCONUT

SERVES 6

1 ¼ cups split red lentils
3 ½ cups spring water
3 tbsp extra virgin olive oil
2 large purple garlic cloves, sliced
2 large onions, diced
2 carrots, sliced
2 leeks, cut into 1-inch slices
1 daikon radish, weighing about ¼ lb, diced
½ tsp ground cinnamon
½ tsp mustard seeds
½ tsp ground or crushed cumin seeds
1 tbsp shredded coconut
½ oz fresh gingerroot, peeled and grated
salt and freshly ground black pepper

Thoroughly rinse the lentils in cold water. Drain.

Bring the spring water to a boil and add the lentils. Bring back to a boil, stirring constantly. Season, cover, and simmer until the lentils are cooked, about 45 minutes. Drain.

Toward the end of the lentil cooking time, place a large heavy pan over medium heat. Pour in the olive oil, then add the garlic and sauté it briefly. Add all the vegetables and sauté them 5 minutes. Add the cinnamon, mustard seeds, cumin, coconut, and fresh ginger. Stir 2 minutes.

Gently stir the vegetable and spice mixture into the drained lentils. Adjust the seasoning, heat through, and serve.

STUFFED EGGPLANT

SERVES 6

6 large eggplants
4 tbsp extra virgin olive oil
1 large purple garlic clove, minced
6 anchovy fillets
1 tsp herbes de Provence
¼ lb tomatoes, peeled, seeded, and coarsely chopped
⅔ cup diced onions
½ cup minced Greek olives (Kalamata)
4 cups fresh whole wheat bread crumbs
salt and freshly ground black pepper

Preheat the oven to 400°F and line a baking sheet with foil.

Cut the eggplants in half lengthwise. Using a small teaspoon, scoop out the eggplant flesh, leaving about ¼ inch of flesh under the skin and taking care not to break the skin at any point.

Spread the scooped-out flesh on the prepared baking sheet and bake 30 minutes.

Meanwhile, brush the flesh left in the eggplant shells with some of the olive oil and then sprinkle with salt. Place the shells in a baking dish and bake for the last 15 minutes with the scooped-out flesh.

Toward the end of this time, heat the remaining oil in a sauté pan over medium heat and add the garlic, anchovies, herbs, tomatoes, and onions. Sauté lightly 3–5 minutes.

Blend these to a smooth purée, then mix this well with the chopped olives and baked eggplant flesh. Season this mixture and use it to stuff the shells. Sprinkle the tops with the bread crumbs.

Bake the stuffed eggplant halves 10–15 minutes and then serve immediately.

*Left: Red Lentils with Cinnamon and Coconut;
right: Stuffed Eggplant*

SCARLET CABBAGE WITH CELERIAC AND APPLE

SERVES 6

2 heads of red cabbage
⅔ cup cider vinegar
1 large baking apple
1 head of celeriac
8 juniper berries, crushed
½ tsp freshly grated nutmeg
2 tbsp concentrated apple juice
3 tbsp butter
salt and freshly ground black pepper

Cut the cabbage heads in half and remove the hard core and any large ribs from the outer leaves. Wash, drain, and pat dry, then slice thinly.

Put 3 quarts of salted water in a large pan and bring to a boil. Place the sliced cabbage in a large colander. Pour the boiling water all over the cabbage. This will turn it deep purple.

Drain thoroughly, then transfer the cabbage to a bowl large enough for it to be thoroughly tossed. Sprinkle with the cider vinegar, making sure that all the cabbage is well coated. The cabbage will now turn bright red.

Preheat the oven to 350°F.

Peel the apple and celeriac, then grate both into a bowl. Add the juniper berries and the nutmeg and mix thoroughly. Stir in the apple concentrate.

Transfer the cabbage to an ovenproof dish, shaking off the cider vinegar. Mix the apple and celeriac mixture into the cabbage. Dot with the butter and adjust the seasoning, if necessary.

Bake 15 minutes. Stir well and bake 10 minutes longer, then toss thoroughly and serve.

Left: Scarlet Cabbage with Celeriac and Apple; right: Onion Chrysanthemums with Gruyère

ONION CHRYSANTHEMUMS WITH GRUYÈRE

SERVES 4

8 large red onions, unpeeled
⅔ cup sunflower seeds
1½ cups Gruyère cheese, grated

Preheat the oven to 400°F.

If necessary, trim the base of the onions, losing as little as possible of the outer skin, so that they will stand upright.

With a sharp knife, make a cut in the top of the onion to about halfway down. Rotate the onion by about 45 degrees and make another cut, perpendicular to the first, in the same way. Repeat this process, trimming and cutting, twice more, to cut into eighths.

Gently pry open the sections of the onion created by the cuts, without breaking any of the "petals" thus formed. Sprinkle the seeds between the "petals," followed by two-thirds of the cheese.

Press the "petals" shut and cover the top of each onion with a small foil "hat." Place the onions in a baking dish.

Bake 45 minutes, removing the foil for the last 5 minutes. Sprinkle with the remaining cheese and serve.

Note: This dish will work well with most hard cheeses, such as Emmental, sharp Cheddar, Jarlsberg, or fresh Parmesan. The sunflower seeds can also be replaced by poppy seeds, pumpkin seeds, fennel seeds, or pine nuts, or even with chopped toasted nuts, such as almonds, walnuts, or hazelnuts.

PINTO BEANS WITH LIME AND CHILI

SERVES 4

2⅓ cups dried pinto beans, soaked overnight
1 tbsp canola oil
1 large carrot, sliced
1 large onion, diced
½ tsp hot chili powder
3 tbsp tahini paste
3 tbsp filtered honey
½ tsp grated zest and juice from a washed lime
salt and freshly ground black pepper

Drain the beans, cover them with fresh cold water, and bring to a boil. Drain and cover again with more fresh water. Bring to a boil once more and simmer until tender, 50–60 minutes. Drain.

Toward the end of this cooking time, heat the oil in a large frying pan, add the carrot and onion, and sauté until tender. Add the chili powder, tahini, and honey. Stir thoroughly and remove from the heat.

Add the beans to the vegetables. Pour in the lime juice and sprinkle with the zest. Mix gently and reheat briefly. Season and transfer to a warmed dish.

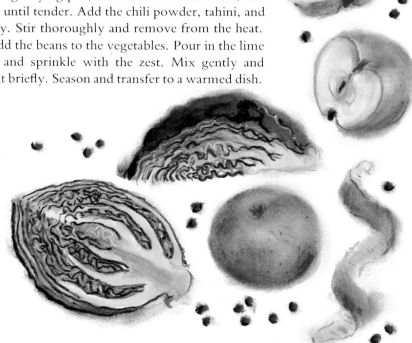

Fresh
POMEGRANATE
seeds are widely
used in salads and
vegetable purées in
the Middle East.
Dried seeds are
often available
when the fresh fruit
is more difficult to
obtain.

BELGIAN ENDIVE, BLUE CHEESE, AND POMEGRANATE SALAD

SERVES 4

4 large heads of Belgian endive
1 pomegranate
2 cups bean sprouts
3 oz blue cheese, such as Gorgonzola or Danish Blue
4 small garlic cloves, minced
⅔ cup Basic Vinaigrette (see page 12)

Pull the Belgian endive leaves apart and arrange them in a salad bowl. (Break them in pieces if they are very large, but do not cut with a knife as this causes bruising and the base of the leaf turns pink.)

Cut the pomegranate in half and pull out the fleshy seeds with a spoon. Mix the bean sprouts with the endive and then crumble the blue cheese over the top. Sprinkle with the pomegranate seeds.

Mix garlic into vinaigrette and dress salad just before serving.

Left: Leafy Green and Red Greek Salad (page 46); right: Belgian Endive, Blue Cheese, and Pomegranate Salad

Any combination of leaves may be used in the LEAFY GREEN AND RED GREEK SALAD, such as Romaine with Oakleaf or Red Leaf.

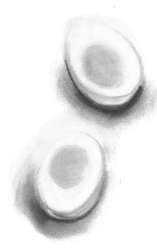

LEAFY GREEN AND RED GREEK SALAD

SERVES 6

1 head of radicchio
1 head of Oakleaf lettuce
1 head of curly endive
¼ lb feta cheese, crumbled into large pieces
⅔ cup Greek olives, pitted and chopped
⅔ cup Low-Calorie Yogurt Dressing (see page 12)
chopped fresh chives, for garnish

Break all the leaves into a salad bowl and mix them together. Add the cheese followed by the olives. Toss with the dressing and garnish with chives.

ROASTED PEPPERS WITH POPPY-SEED DRESSING

SERVES 4

3 large red sweet peppers
3 large green sweet peppers
1 tbsp poppy seeds
2 tbsp chopped mixed fresh herbs, including chives, chervil, parsley, and tarragon
⅔ cup French Vinaigrette (see page 12)

Preheat the oven to 450°F or preheat the broiler.

Roast the whole peppers in the oven or under the broiler until the skin blisters and turns black. Cover them with a damp linen cloth and let them cool.

Once cool, peel the charred skins from the peppers, over a bowl in order to catch any juices.

Discard the seeds and white pith from inside the peppers and slice the flesh into long thick strips. Arrange these in a shallow serving dish.

Stir any pepper juices, the poppy seeds, and herbs into the dressing and pour this over the peppers before serving.

SPINACH SALAD WITH EGGS AND CROUTONS

SERVES 4

1 lb young spinach leaves
3 eggs, hard-cooked
3 stalks of celery, cut into slices about ¼-inch thick
Cheese Croutons (see page 17)
¾ cup freshly grated Parmesan cheese
2 tbsp milk
⅔ cup Hollandaise Sauce (see page 11)
salt and freshly ground black pepper

Remove any stems and coarse ribs from the spinach.

Separate the egg yolks from the whites. Slice the whites finely and push the yolks thorough a strainer.

Tear the spinach leaves into a bowl. Add the celery followed by the croutons and toss gently. Add the egg whites followed by the Parmesan.

Stir the milk into the hollandaise sauce, adjust the seasoning, and pour it over the salad. Sprinkle with the egg yolks, toss, and serve.

BROWN RICE SALAD WITH ORANGE, SAGE, AND DATES

SERVES 4

1 washed orange
1 tbsp finely chopped fresh young sage leaves
⅔ cup coarsely chopped dates
3 cups cooked brown rice

FOR THE CASHEW–NUT DRESSING

½ cup low-fat cream cheese
1 ½ tbsp cashew nut oil
1 ½ tbsp lemon juice
1 ½ tbsp coarse salt
freshly ground black pepper
2–3 tbsp Homemade Mayonnaise (see page 11)
½ cup chopped cashew nuts

Pare off the zest from the orange, avoiding any of the bitter white pith, and cut it into thin julienne strips. Stir together with the sage and dates into the rice.

Make the dressing: Blend the cream cheese, with the oil, lemon juice, salt, and pepper. Fold in the mayonnaise, followed by the nuts. If the dressing is too thick, thin it with 1–2 tablespoons of low-fat milk. Toss the salad with the dressing and serve.

SHRIMP AND SHIITAKE MUSHROOM SALAD

SERVES 4

¼ lb dried shiitake mushrooms
¼ lb Chinese egg noodles, cooked
bunch of large scallions, sliced,
(including the green tops)
½ lb corn salad (mâche)
freshly ground black pepper
¼ lb peeled cooked small shrimp
1 ½ tbsp soy sauce
1 ½ tbsp Japanese rice vinegar
3 ½ tbsp black sesame seeds, toasted

Soak the mushrooms in water 30 minutes, then drain and squeeze out any excess liquid. Discarding any hard pieces of stem, snip the mushrooms into small pieces with kitchen scissors.

Place the noodles in a salad bowl, then add the mushrooms, scallions, and corn salad. Toss lightly, season with pepper, and add the shrimp.

Dress with a little of the soy sauce and rice vinegar, then sprinkle with toasted sesame seeds.

Chill 15 minutes before serving, dressed with the remaining soy sauce and vinegar.

SHIITAKE MUSHROOMS *have been cultivated by the Japanese on oak bark for centuries. Dried shiitakes are widely available in gourmet food stores and some supermarkets. They must be soaked in water for 30 minutes before use and stems trimmed off.*

The sweet and delicate flavor of JAPANESE RICE VINEGAR *is an essential part of many traditional dishes, such as fish sushi. Light cider vinegar may be substituted.*

Any combination of the wide range of salad leaves and fresh herbs now available will make a good salad. Try replacing the lettuce with watercress, the spinach with corn salad, and using chervil and tarragon instead of dill.

SALADE NATURELLE AUX FINES HERBES

SERVES 4–6

1 large head of romaine or iceberg lettuce
1 fennel bulb
1 head of Belgian endive
1 package of mustard and cress sprouts
½ lb young spinach leaves, coarsely chopped
½ English cucumber, diced
1 ½ tbsp capers
1 ½ cups diced cooked potatoes
1 large onion, diced
1 tbsp chopped fresh dill
1 tbsp chopped fresh parsley
¼ lb smoked salmon, cut into thin strips
6 tbsp olive oil
2 tbsp Japanese rice vinegar
coarse salt
freshly ground black pepper
1 tbsp chopped fresh chives, for garnish
4 nasturtium flowers, for garnish

Separate the lettuce leaves into a large salad bowl. Pull apart the leaves of the fennel and Belgian endive and slice them. Add the fennel, endive, and spinach to the lettuce.

Toss the cucumber, capers, potatoes, onion, dill, and parsley together in a smaller bowl. Place this mixture in the center of the salad and toss in the smoked salmon.

Blend together the oil and vinegar with salt and pepper. Pour over the salad and toss well.

Garnish with the chives and nasturtium flowers and serve immediately.

Left: Shrimp and Shiitake Mushroom Salad (page 47);
right: Salade Naturelle aux Fines Herbes

In Quail Egg and Smoked Salmon Salad, smoked trout or thinly sliced raw tuna will work well as substitutes for smoked salmon.

QUAIL EGG AND SMOKED SALMON SALAD

SERVES 6

bunch of watercress, stems removed
2 cooked beets, thinly sliced
1 head of romaine or oak leaf lettuce
¼ lb smoked salmon, cut into thin strips
3 tbsp butter
6 quail eggs
freshly ground black pepper
⅔ cup Basic Vinaigrette (see page 12)
sprigs of fresh dill, for garnish (optional)
1 large lemon, cut into 6 wedges, for serving

Place the watercress in little piles in the middle of 6 salad plates. Arrange the beet slices around the watercress.

Tear the lettuce leaves into small pieces and arrange them in a ring around the outside of the beet slices.

Arrange 2 strips of smoked salmon in a criss-cross on top of each pile of watercress and arrange the rest around the outside of the rings of lettuce.

Melt the butter in a frying pan over medium heat and fry the quail eggs briefly until the white is just set. Sprinkle them with black pepper and then arrange one egg on top of each pile of watercress.

Dress the leaves and beets with the vinaigrette and serve immediately, garnished with dill sprigs, if using. Serve the lemon wedges separately for the salmon.

SUMMERHOUSE SALAD WITH ORANGE VINAIGRETTE

SERVES 6

1 large head of romaine or Oakleaf lettuce
bunch of watercress, stems removed
2 large avocados
2 large pears, peeled and sliced
1 cup coarsely chopped cooked chicken breast
FOR THE ORANGE VINAIGRETTE
1 tbsp freshly squeezed orange juice, including some flesh
⅔ cup Basic Vinaigrette (see page 12)
salt and freshly ground black pepper

Separate the lettuce leaves into a salad bowl, add the watercress, and toss gently.

Halve and pit the avocados. Using a small spoon, scoop out the advocado flesh and add this to the salad.

Chop the pear slices into the salad and arrange the pieces of chicken on top.

Stir the orange juice and flesh into the basic vinaigrette and adjust the seasoning, if necessary. Pour this over the salad and serve.

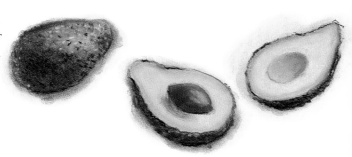

Left: Summerhouse Salad with Orange Vinaigrette; right: Corn Salad with Mango and Hazelnuts (page 53)

CORN SALAD WITH MANGO AND HAZELNUTS

SERVES 4

1 large ripe mango
¾ lb corn salad (mâche)
1 cup toasted hazelnuts
3 tbsp crème fraîche or sour cream
1 tbsp pickled green peppercorns
1 tsp lime juice
salt and freshly ground black pepper

Peel and pit the mango and coarsely chop the flesh.

Place the corn salad in a salad bowl. Sprinkle the hazelnuts over this and arrange the mango on top.

Mix the crème fraîche with the peppercorns and lime juice. Season and pour over the salad. Toss at the table and serve immediately.

BABY SWEET CORN AND SNOW PEA SALAD

SERVES 4

½ lb snow peas
½ lb baby sweet corn
½ cup sliced almonds
½ cup chopped hazelnuts
2 tbsp hazelnut oil, warmed
salt and freshly ground black pepper

Plunge the snow peas and baby sweet corn into a pan of boiling salted water and blanch 2 minutes. Drain and refresh in cold water. Pat dry and let cool.

Place the vegetables in a salad bowl and mix in the nuts. Season the warmed hazelnut oil and pour it over the salad.

Left: Baby Sweet Corn and Snow Pea Salad; right: Chanterelle Salad with Basil Vinaigrette

CHANTERELLE SALAD WITH BASIL VINAIGRETTE

SERVES 4

2 sprigs of fresh thyme
salt
1 lb fresh chanterelle mushrooms
1 recipe Cheese Croutons (see page 17)
2 large purple garlic cloves, minced
6 large fresh basil leaves, chopped
¼ cup Basic Vinaigrette (see page 12)
¼ cup minced fresh parsley, for garnish

Place the thyme in a pan and add 2 cups of water with some salt. Bring to a boil and boil 5 minutes.

Add the mushrooms, cover, and reduce the heat. Simmer gently 5 minutes. Discard the thyme, drain the mushrooms, and let them cool.

Place the cooled mushrooms and the croutons in a salad bowl and toss lightly. Combine the garlic and basil with the vinaigrette, then drizzle over the salad. Garnish with parsley and serve immediately.

CORN SALAD WITH MANGO AND HAZELNUTS *can be made using other exotic fruits, such as papaya or pineapple, instead of mango.*

The recipe for CHANTERELLE SALAD *can be adapted and made with common mushrooms, but it will not have the same flavor.*

SIDE DISHES

*E*ven the most adventurous of cooks is quite likely to serve plain boiled, steamed, or baked vegetables as side dishes to accompany main courses. Although there is nothing wrong with this no-nonsense approach, there are also many wonderfully easy ways to make vegetable accompaniments into little feasts on their own without really spending much more time, money, or effort. It may be as simple as tossing in some chopped fresh herbs or a few toasted nuts with a bit of butter just before serving, or an unusual and attractive means of presentation, such as the *String Bean Bouquets,* or perhaps a novel way of cooking a traditional favorite, like *Deep-Fried Parsley.* Many of the recipes that follow, as well as being capable of enlivening the plainest of main courses, are also colorful and interesting enough to be used as appetizers, snacks, or light meals in their own right.

Left to right: Braised Red Onions (page 56); Herbed Carrots Tossed in Lemon Mayonnaise (page 57); Stir-Fried Zucchini (page 56)

Chinese HOISIN SAUCE *is made from soybeans and is flavored with chili peppers, garlic, and rice vinegar. Its sweet flavor works well with vegetables and meat dishes and is particularly suited to barbecue sauces.*

BRAISED RED ONIONS

SERVES 4

2 tbsp butter
4 large red onions, thinly sliced
salt and freshly ground black pepper

Melt the butter in a heavy pan over medium heat. Add the onions and cook gently until translucent.

Season, then cover and simmer over very low heat about 20 minutes. Stir and transfer to a warmed serving dish.

MUSHROOMS WITH HOISIN SAUCE

SERVES 4

1 lb flat, open mushrooms
2 tbsp butter
1 tbsp extra virgin olive oil
salt and freshly ground black pepper
juice of ½ lemon
2 tbsp hoisin sauce
2 tbsp chopped fresh cilantro

Clean the mushrooms well, but do not wash them.

Melt the butter with the oil in a heavy frying pan over medium-low heat and toss the mushrooms, until well coated. Cook gently until tender.

Transfer the mushrooms to a warmed serving plate, leaving the juices in the pan. Season the juices and stir in the lemon juice and hoisin sauce.

Pour this over the mushrooms and sprinkle with the coriander before serving.

STIR-FRIED ZUCCHINI

SERVES 4

2 tbsp butter
2 tbsp light soy sauce
freshly ground black pepper
8 zucchini, thickly sliced

Melt the butter in a large frying pan over medium heat. Add the soy sauce and some black pepper, followed by the zucchini. Stir the zucchini to coat them evenly in the seasoned butter. Cover the pan and cook over medium heat 5 minutes, shaking the pan frequently.

Transfer to a warmed serving dish.

HERBED CARROTS TOSSED IN LEMON MAYONNAISE

SERVES 4

1 lb carrots, scrubbed, unpeeled, and cut into disks about
¹/₂-inch thick
2 tsp herbes de Provence
¹/₂ tsp grated zest and 1 tsp juice from a washed lemon
1 tbsp mayonnaise
salt and freshly ground black pepper

Place the carrots in a pan that has a tight-fitting lid. Barely cover with water and add the herbs.

Cover the pan and cook over medium heat until just tender, 15–20 minutes. Shake the pan frequently and add more water from time to time if necessary. Drain, stir in the other ingredients, and season.

POTATOES WITH DANDELION GREENS AND TOMATO SAUCE

SERVES 4

¹/₂ lb potatoes in their skins
salt
¹/₂ lb dandelion greens
4 tomatoes, thinly sliced
¹/₄ cup coarsely chopped stuffed green olives
1 cup warm Quick Tomato Sauce (see page 10)

In a large pan of boiling salted water, cook the potatoes until tender. Drain, let cool slightly, and then slice. Keep warm.

Blanch greens 20 seconds only in boiling salted water. Refresh in cold water, drain, and pat dry.

Arrange the greens in a serving dish and cover with the tomato slices. Sprinkle with olives, arrange the potato slices on top, and pour over the sauce.

STUFFED TOMATOES

SERVES 2

2 large beefsteak tomatoes
1 tbsp butter
¹/₂ tbsp extra virgin olive oil
1 purple garlic clove, minced
1 large onion, coarsely chopped
salt and freshly ground black pepper
1 tbsp chopped fresh parsley
1 tbsp chopped fresh chives
2 oz feta cheese, cubed

Preheat the oven to 375°F.

Cut the tops from the tomatoes and reserve them. Scoop out the seeds and pulp to leave an empty cavity in each tomato.

Melt the butter with the oil in a sauté pan over medium heat and add the garlic. Sauté 2 minutes, then add the onion and cook until tender. Season, then sprinkle the parsley and chives into the onions. Stir, then immediately remove from the heat.

Stuff each of the tomatoes with the onion mixture. Then top that filling with the cheese and replace the tops.

Bake 30 minutes, and serve hot.

Small tender DANDELION GREENS *can be gathered wild in the early part of the year; they are also grown commercially. They go well in salads with chopped bacon and ham.*

STRING BEAN BOUQUETS

SERVES 4

1 lb fine string beans
bunch of fresh chives
½ canned pimiento, drained and cut into long
thin strips
6 tbsp butter
½ lemon
coarse salt
freshly ground black pepper

Trim all the beans to the same length, leaving the tails on some if necessary.

Plunge the beans into a large pan of boiling salted water and simmer 3–6 minutes, depending on the preferred degree of firmness. Drain and refresh under cold running water. Drain well and pat dry.

In the same water, blanch the chives 30 seconds only. Refresh, drain, and pat dry.

Separate the beans into 6 bundles and tie them together with 2 chives per bundle, securing with two knots. Loop the pimiento strips decoratively around the bundles.

Melt the butter in a frying pan over low heat, then carefully roll the bundles in it until they are thoroughly heated through.

Place on a warmed serving plate. Squeeze the lemon juice over the bundles, then sprinkle with salt and pepper.

Note: You can do this sort of ornamental serving with a wide range of vegetables, such as asparagus spears and young leeks. Tying up may also be effected with scallion greens or leek tops that have been cut into long thin strips and blanched. Blanched strips of apple peel or zest from oranges, lemons, and limes are also attractive and provide interesting color to vegetable side dishes.

JAPANESE PICKLED VEGETABLES

SERVES 4

1 head of cauliflower, separated into florets
1 small daikon radish, peeled and sliced
2 carrots, sliced
½ large cucumber, peeled and sliced
1 tsp sugar
pinch of salt
about 2 cups Japanese rice vinegar

Slice the cauliflower florets thinly lengthwise into thin slices. Arrange the cauliflower slices together with the slices of daikon, carrot, and cucumber on a flat serving dish or in a bowl.

Dissolve the sugar and salt in the rice vinegar and pour this over the vegetables. Cover with plastic wrap and marinate 12 hours in the refrigerator.

To serve, drain the pieces of vegetable, reserving the marinade for later use with more vegetables. Arrange in a serving dish.

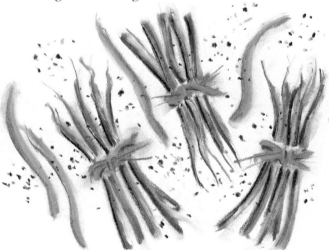

Top: String Bean Bouquets; bottom: Japanese Pickled Vegetables

BABY BRUSSELS SPROUTS WITH PINE NUTS

SERVES 4

1 lb baby Brussels sprouts
½ tbsp hazelnut oil
⅔ cup pine nuts
salt and freshly ground black pepper

Steam the sprouts 3 minutes over boiling water, without removing the lid. Remove from the heat.

Put the hazelnut oil in the bottom of a warmed serving dish. Add the pine nuts and salt and pepper, followed by the sprouts.

Toss gently until thoroughly coated with oil and then serve immediately.

CABBAGE WITH CARAWAY SEEDS AND SESAME OIL

SERVES 4

2 tbsp butter
2 tbsp roasted sesame oil
1 tsp caraway seeds
¾ lb head of white cabbage, thinly sliced
salt and freshly ground black pepper

CABBAGE WITH
CARAWAY SEEDS
AND SESAME OIL
*lends itself to many
variations. Try
replacing the
caraway seeds with
poppy seeds, fennel
seeds, or crushed
coriander seeds
mixed with
blanched strips of
zest from washed
orange.*

Melt the butter with the oil in a pan over medium heat. Add the caraway seeds and toss gently 1 minute. Add the cabbage and toss to coat thoroughly with the butter and oil.

Place the lid on the pan and increase the heat. Cook 2–3 minutes only, shaking the pan constantly. Season and transfer to a warmed serving dish. Serve immediately.

Left: Cabbage with Caraway Seeds and Sesame Oil; right: Baby Brussels Sprouts with Pine Nuts

DEEP-FRIED PARSLEY

SERVES 4

6 bunches of curly parsley (with stems)
salt
peanut oil, for deep-frying

Heat the oil to 360°F (a cube of dry bread browns in 60 seconds).

Separate the parsley into 12 equal bunches, tying with kitchen twine to secure. Shake the bunches and dry very thoroughly with paper towels.

Holding the bunches by their stems with wooden tongs, plunge into the hot oil one by one. In a very few seconds (3–5), the heads will shrivel.

Remove while still green and place gently on paper towels. As the parsley cools it becomes crisp.

Season lightly and serve when all are fried.

CHILLED AVOCADOS WITH LIME AND WALNUT SAUCE

SERVES 4

1 oz whole wheat bread crusts (about ¾ cup)
4 large garlic cloves, minced
¾ cup almonds
juice of 4 large limes, flesh included
1 tbsp walnut oil
4 ripe avocados, chilled

Soak crusts in water until softened, then squeeze dry.

Place all the ingredients except the avocados in a blender and pulse gently until well combined. Still pulsing gently, add 1 tablespoon of water, a few drops at a time, to give a creamy consistency.

Peel, halve, and pit the avocados and place in a shallow dish. Pour over the nut sauce to serve.

Deep-Fried Parsley served on radicchio leaves

SAUTÉED CUCUMBER WITH ONIONS AND DILL

SERVES 4

2½ large cucumbers, peeled, halved, and seeded
4 tbsp butter
2 onions, sliced
salt and freshly ground black pepper
1½ tbsp chopped fresh dill

Sprinkle the cucumber pieces with salt and let drain 15 minutes. Rinse, drain, and pat dry.

Bring 2 quarts of lightly salted water to a boil, then add the cucumbers and cook until tender but still firm, 7–10 minutes. Drain and cut into chunks.

Melt the butter in a large heavy pan, add the onions, and cook them gently until just translucent.

Raise the heat and add the cucumber chunks, stirring thoroughly to help any liquid to evaporate. When all the excess liquid is gone, reduce the heat and cook gently 10–15 minutes longer.

Season, add the dill, and toss gently, then serve.

CHILLED AVOCADOS WITH LIME AND WALNUT SAUCE *are delicious served with cold chicken or spicy dishes.*

INDEX

ACKNOWLEDGEMENTS
The Publishers would like to thank the following for the use of accessories in the photography:

Stitches & Daughters,
5–7 Tranquil Vale,
London SE3

The Perfect Glass Shop,
5 Park Walk,
London SW10